Aggregate

ALSO BY GUY BIRCHARD

Baby Grand (Ilderton, Ont.: Brick / Nairn, 1979)
Neckeverse (Newcastle upon Tyne: Galloping Dog Press, 1989)
Birchard's Garage (Durham: Pig Press, 1991)
Travelling Mercies (Bray, Ireland: Wild Honey Press, 1999)
Twenty Grand (Boston, MA.: Pressed Wafer, 2003)
Further than the Blood (Boston, MA: Pressed Wafer, 2010)
Hecatomb (Brooklyn, NY: Pressed Wafer, 2017)

Guy Birchard

Aggregate
: retrospective

Shearsman Books

First published in the United Kingdom in 2018 by
Shearsman Books
50 Westons Hill Drive
Emersons Green
BRISTOL
BS16 7DF

Shearsman Books Ltd Registered Office
30–31 St. James Place, Mangotsfield, Bristol BS16 9JB
(this address not for correspondence)

www.shearsman.com

ISBN 978-1-84861-575-5

ACKNOWLEDGEMENTS

First publication of the series here collected:

Grandmother's Middle Name Was America — *Scripsi*, 1985
Shownman — Brick Books, 1982
Cold Mine — *Grain Magazine*, 1985
Travelling Mercies — Wild Honey Press, 1999

Contents

This reprise is dedicated to staunch Br'er Marsh.

Grandmother's Middle Name Was America

Grandmother's Middle Name Was America was written in Venice, California in the summer of 1979. Wish I could say it sprang from my forehead.

Almost did.

Venice Beach was my office. And academy.

'The Green Mountains…' appeared in *Montreal Writers' Forum* (June 1979).

Grandmother's Middle Name Was America was self-produced that summer as a broadside, about 75 copies, under the aegis of the Beyond Baroque Foundation; appeared in the Australian quarterly *Scripsi* (April 1985) and was collected in *Neckeverse* (Newcastle upon Tyne: Galloping Dog Press, 1989). *Further Than the Blood* (Boston: Pressed Wafer, 2010) includes an excerpt.

The Green Mountains in high summer haze
                    invisible.

Dirt roads lead toward them
                        regardless.

Vapours cling like wet silk.

The woods,
                    creeks and brilliant
            blue
birds alarm
the casual walker.

The ready hiker
holds a steady
course
through obfuscating heat

approaching the near
mountains
                    invisible
through haze.

Dominion Day in America

Cereal
>   waves golden in North
>   American fields.

Dates
>   utter the watchwords
>   of nations, flirting.

Palms
>   crossed with silver
>   once told fortune
>   wave so long.

Mint
>   the cool, milled coin
>   the greenback more or
>   less par.

Tender
>   the border north,
>   south.

Hiroshima Day in America

Alto
stratus
above

the Pacific, sky the

color of morels.

Bright

victory this day...
spots before the eyes

the increase of vain
works, peacetime

permitting,

re revolt never

tholed. Regret glad

tidings:
entente
enfin.

Ring Thy Bell

God's own blue ache
shines in a young
lord's face.

Young Ezra's gold
earring didn't
last. God's

lips smile.
Old

Ezra's purse.

Hiz
plainsong current.

Kempt
or frowzy,
toned or slack, old

testamental Ezra &
God's tempered
Will be done.

The Santa Monica Mountains
            invisible
in high summer

        haze.

Cool sea
breezes blow
wary traveller's cares

awry.

Pelicans glide and dive.

Still
        sand and palm
                        fronds
rest.

The very sun is hid,
drops red
between banks of

        haze.

Shownman

I hero-worshipped braided Grey Owl in earliest childhood—before I did more than study the b/w pictures and covet the buckskins. Years later, in the summer of 1972, I portaged (and paddled) a tatty reading-copy of *Pilgrims of the Wild* from Kenora, Ontario, to Fort Albany, a thousand miles. Anon I collected Firsts and scarce Associations enough to brief his bibliographer.

Grey Owl was natural-born eco-crusader. We feather and foul our own nests, birth and circumstance. How come. To accuse the East Sussex Archie Belaney now, in these hyper-orthodox times, of fraudulence and "cultural appropriation" is pettishly to ignore Grey Owl's point.

Then he died for seclusion.

Shownman (found word from the final Lovat Dickson bio, a typo there) was largely written in Vancouver in 1980, a crucial section on a bench by Stanley Park's Beaver Lake—where else.

The last section of *Shownman* happened to be the first written—with no hunch that there would be any more to it—thus 'I can be good company' appeared in *Brick* 6 (Spring, 1979); in the chapbook *Baby Grand* (Ilderton, Ont.: Brick / Nairn, 1979); and again in *Brick* 12 (Spring, 1981).

Eventually *Shownman* appeared entire in the anthology *News and Weather: Seven Canadian Poets* (Ilderton: Brick Books, 1982). It was collected in *Neckeverse*.

Once more, in 2000, 'I can be good company' appeared in the anthology *New Life in Dark Seas: Brick Books 25*.

'The Trigger in the Trees' was excerpted in *Further Than the Blood*.

To me the rifle has ever been mightier than the pen.

Archie Belaney, Grey
Owl

not Mohawk Oneida
Onondaga
Cayuga Seneca nor
Tuscarora not Iroquois

neither Five nor Six
Nations

never no Huron.

Montagnais nope
Naskapi
Cree
Têtes-de-Boules nor
Penobscot
Micmac or Abenaki.

No Apache, no.

By adoption: Ojibway.

The chrysalis moot—
British Tex-
Mex Scot or
Canuck

son of Katherine
Cochise or Cox and MacNeil,
rake or hero,
friend of Buffalo
Bill's or fan.

Born at Hastings or
Hermosillo, Bear
Island, Ajawaan
Lake...

It's never late till morning and then it's early.

Archibald Stansfeld Belaney changed his
name, race and serial
number.

Faded into dense bush.

Emerged river-born,
guiding a divinity
student in the bow of his canoe.

No clashing of cymbals
but the roaring dictate
of the rapids taught this
seminarian
his first lesson in fear-of-the-lord

so throwing down
the paddle
he clasped hands in
supplication—

shite & white water.

*Quit your fool
babbling and get that paddle, man—
when you're in my
canoe I*

am your Lord.

Bad Hat

The young hellion balanced
hatchet prowess with Shakespeare
and Browning, the accent
on throwing-knives and such stunts.

The girls must go home
giddy from dancing to Archie's
piano and drum fandangos,
his fingers' touch still tight on their ribs,
their perfume and whisky blanc
still high in his nose.

The Station Agent and the Bay
Factor pasted and frightened,
the Law down from Chapleau,
strangers who laugh out of line,
elder citizens requiring
their peace

       made him brood.

He was never penitent.
Always the bloody knives or the Browning
got him in trouble in town.
When he left there he shot at both churches.
Two bells in their steeples rang from his bullets.

Too-True Tall Tales

I'll walk across Algonquin Park in the dark
and I'll carry my gun all the way.
I'll do it in the freezing
night if I can't get across in a day
and I'll do it cold,
        light no blessed fire
drawing Rangers to catch me if I tire.

You bet—I'll dare
        and I'll collect.

        But the goddam ice was thin
and like the greenhorn I haven't been
since 17 I stepped in it past my boot
all right   past my bloody knee.

Then I went fast
though the leggings freezing chafed
the skin of my groin
and my toes went numb   too right
        my feet   I couldn't feel.
I was falling off my very snowshoes.

But I kept my gun

and I kept travelling
and never lit no fire
though I could've and might as well've
because yes he picked up my trail.

'Twas a rumour
                he caught, mind,
                        never a scent.

27

He found me too and I thank him, and Him twice.
I'd drifted asleep into that peculiar
sleep you may fall into only once.

Part cat I am—with eight lives I left
his Ranger's roost after a fortnight
and not a toe did I lose

till I left my traps and went to trenches
and Jerry shot 'em off in the Great War.

Hell, them bastards
only ever got me by accident.

The Trigger in the Trees

Cuss softly
only at trivia that breath
be saved.

Squeeze
the trigger in the trees.

Burn the beaver's
knees to make amends.

Put tobacco in the bear
skull's brainpan.
Hang her on a limb to witness
man's poor awe.

Hard years to learn
seasons' easy lessons:

the best thing you can do in summer
is marry,
fight fire or show Americans where
pike bask.

Pray for bitter winters: cold
best conditions ice
and snow for shoe and toboggan.

Ignore the dying black and yellow
eyes. Bloody forearms.
Admire the flayed sable fur.

                              Then,
where the disappearing creatures
could be found to kill, my wife
refused to follow.

A wed woman and a caught
lynx conspired.
The Beaver People wanted
much. They made live
            music.

The cudgel started turning in my hands.

Bewildered, our eyes
began to meet in Silent Places.

Saints and man conversed at mid-
night and noon of earthly
ways and profanity.

      Traps'
weight drowns
            creation.

      He hefts a pencil
to trace the past for vice and assent.

      ...these writings that were no longer mine, but which I now saw only as
recorded echoes and not creations of my own, had captured the essentials of
what had eluded me so long.
      And I felt at last that I had been made to understand.

Alba: England

All night I'll stand till day
breaks and from dawn
I'll stand till the day begins.

I'll prove all the patience of a life-
time in the pitch-dark hours
men dream through.

Snowblind, I could find
the cover of the pines
by ear and stand the storm.

I can with foreboding
behold my fame
unproclaimed.

Perhaps come morning
that publisher entrusts me with the lore
a writer needs to thrive in London?

Faces like a forest
                    listening.

Lecterns fit the hand like thwart
                    and haft.

Applause like relief at the end of a carry
heavy in increments of disillusion.

Backstage they beg,
                    Please be
"Saint-Francis-of-the-Beavers"—
and the appeal of a woman with a knowing eye
is great. A fool's fists are flies.
A water glass full of whisky, if you
please.

The obscure woods are better.
Oaths keep better.
That pilgrimage would be good to make
again.

     But oh God

the forest back down
the way none may go

there the only
nourishment and service.

     Now

     the land and family
     finally estranged.

At a Command Performance
                              the performer
readies himself on stage at the pleasure
                              of the Royal
entourage.
                    When he has waited
Their Majesties enter.

He may never relax.

Noblesse Sauvage n'oblige personne.

                    You, Your
                    Majesties,
                    be seated
                    first

                    then command
                    my entrance.

                    I will not keep you waiting…

                    I will be there
                    instanter.

                              ❀

As the Princesses bid me
I will linger. The children hear
my tales of the Height of Land in storied
Far Away where the water falls
white as age from eminence to
eminence…

We will take tea in frocks and buckskins,
then say farewell,
and I will clap their father on the shoulder
and call him brother.

I can be good company, Grey Owl
sighed,

      where he had no company.

A woman on the CP line through Biscotasing
bares old scars Archie gave her
with the point of his knife. She remembers him
taking to the wild.

      Her eyes glitter,
invite memory:

      how to survive midwinter nights
      with a single blanket, a lean-to
      of boughs and a small fire, how to
      stay alive all those hours

      how to travel the rapids *by night,*
      how to trap at all?

I live for the small, 'live things.
They are my living, to whom
I credit my life. Their pelts
are worth more than yours and mine.
Still, sir, I bow to you and, madam,

I am charmed.

Cold Mine

It occurred to me in a dream that I might write this formative story of my father's adolescence, one he himself fastidiously preferred to obscure. I regretted that I knew so few words with which objectively to tell it. He regretted this many. In the end **Cold Mine** was acceptable to him—mostly. I think.

Aspiring to epical jeroboam, I started the writing in a rooming-house in Montreal's McGill Ghetto in the spring of 1981—by and by on San Francisco's Nob Hill to conclude with this scant naggin of distillate.

High proof though...

Cold Mine (bankrolled by friend Tom ("Montague Trust") Curry, who had prospered) was self-produced as a chapbook printed by the Bednarczyks at Poets and Painters Press in London in 1983 before it appeared in the Canadian magazine *Grain* in February 1985. It was excerpted (poorly) in the anthology *Louis Zukofsky, or whoever someone else thought he was: a collection of responses to the work of L.Z.* (Twickenham: North & South Press, 1988). (*Cold Mine*'s moves owe more to Brent MacKay, *King of Bean*, Brick Books, 1981.) It was collected in *Neckeverse*—and excerpted in *Blood*.

Nobody reported taking a scunner to *Cold Mine*. But nobody loved it to death either. It did win token approbatory murmurs from, like, George Woodcock, Guy Davenport, Northrop Frye, Kenneth Cox. The odd misreader recoiled from standing corrected. Many recipients stayed mum. For instance, disappointingly, William Cookson, who possibly figured the booklet consciously copped Agenda's look. That was inadvertent. Honest. Anyway I gave away, or foisted, pretty well all 250 copies, 35 years ago, and to this day you can still score one easy from abe, cheap—author's signed card bearing warm personal greetings to illuminatus laid in.

In the spring of 1984, Marsh Birchard produced a 16mm colour film of brother G. reading *Cold Mine* on a sound-stage in Toronto. It has never been screened.

summer '29 the hand-
work began by shovel
and barrow to open
another's abandoned
cold mine

prospects: a living—trade
for coal a garden tractor,
celery, pork, beef,
the family's first
Stromberg-Carlson for coal

ton for ton

husband and wife both
bent underground
tunnelled and shoved
the first haul out

raised their own
shotgun shack, kids
and garden in the broad
coulee bottom

hired men came to bunk
led elder sons out of
school to labour

she moved the younger
brood to town—he
trekked weekly the two miles
toting groceries in knee-deep
snow without skis or skid

grading a road up the steep
coulee incline with a horse-drawn maintainer
the rig rolled
horses and all in a tangle of
traces and hooves

lucky the animals unharmed
the embarrassed drayman ravelled
the maze of harness lines to save
cutting them

quick hitched the team
once more

access north to highway,
provide the neighbour
coal to cross his fields

fight the neighbour west
for right-of-way direct to town

pay the government, one dollar
per acre for mineral
rights and royalties
@ ten cents the ton

market the soft
slow burning lignite,
three bucks the ton at best

sell cheap in summer
stockpiled and dehydrating, $1.50

Slope Mine

deific timbered
lightless arch
entrance:

miners scuttle after carbide-
lit horizon till it
flares against

the face too low to stand
before, pitch-dark
filthy wet and chill

pry in headlamp's hiss
and breath's mist carboniferous
matter back to life

two-by-fours on edge
form track, the wheels of the cars
tireless rims

the shores green poplar
saplings, no butt over 6" in diameter
restraining all the earth above

five tons a day a collier could shift

stymied by a solid seam
he'd wrap a pick handle with paper,
roll a tube in which to pour black powder
sufficient for the size of shot required

drill a 2" hole 4 to 6' into the vein,
ram in a steel pipe,
pack it in with clay and rock detritus

snug the charge with a tamping bar
tight down the deep end of the pipe
and fire a squib into it

as the chambers quake exit
till the gases vent

blast ruptured artesian stream
threatened mine with flood
too heavy for worn one-lung pump engine
overburdened already with mere ground-
water

Grandfather corked the fountain
pounded a length of green poplar against
the gush it shot back out over and over
before it swelled and
held

together in the bunkhouse
someone removed his dentures
and a stranger watching,
a newcomer with no English,
gibbered and wept

years later he recollected

> *I never seen false teeth in anyone before*
> *when the teeth came out like that*
> *I thought he was falling apart*
> *I thought his face coming to pieces*
> *in front of my eyes*

Friday night bath water
after so many souls, too black
for the last to bother

odd days modest men
stripped and showered in
downpours

safety inspector propositioned
bumpkin

fifteen she shy of denying intended
not to tryst nor tell
big brother miners

for days evaded
suitor about town

Shaft Mine

Birchard paces uphill
surveying by feel eye
and string-length
reckoning in the grass
and sun the slope
the corresponding
depth and direction
his mine takes in the clay

finally halts
having divined
nothing just
figgered

tells his sons, *Sink
'er here*

curious fossils kicked from the drill wrack
mother-of-pearl in the lode saved
corkscrew patterns in the rock fingered

elated
breaks through right at the face
65' from surface to stope

clutch engaged Ford motor
powered windlass wound rope
around discarded thresher cylinder
bearings greased, only weld
flanges to guide cable

hoisted hopper as per former
grain elevator function
heaped at pit bottom
self-emptied at surface
spilled over jamb in derrick
down chute into waiting wagon
while customer's team grazed
he socialized, satisfied, serviced

the pyramidal tipple
fashioned of beams, planks, pulleys
topped the crib miners climbed down
and clambered from to quit

economy and climate
decade dead revived

culture and nature compared notes

flatlanders' choices multiplied

mine face for battlefront
rough tools for Ross rifles

grain more gold than coal

hardware swapped for seed
shafts collapsed and sealed

the equipment improvised
and engineered from scrap, scrap
again

as children a body's length
belly-down crawl space
still existed

we called the site Indian
Rocks *and knew nothing*
of mine or reminiscence

the generations succeed
divulging little

pick up
a lump of coal
spit on it
toss it over the left
shoulder, don't watch
where it falls:

good luck

Travelling Mercies

I thought the manner of **Travelling Mercies** would repeat *Cold Mine*. In the event, it came off journalistically, almost travelogue—only more transcendent, if we're lucky—and disjunctive enough to defy much revision here. So stet—though the copulative remains the ideal.

I had always wanted to see what was over the horizon many hundreds of miles straight south of Saskatchewan's Willow Bunch Lake country where Heeney & I kept the Shack in the ghost town the spear side of my family had inhabited decades before—so on my 40th birthday we headed out...

Ten years later, in 1999, *Travelling Mercies* was published as a chapbook by Wild Honey Press in Bray, Ireland—and was excerpted in *Blood* another decade after that.

A Cristofre on his brest of silver shene

In a world complimented so lavishly by such as J. Frank Dobie, Wallace Stegner, Merrill Gilfillan, their excellent kind, I remark simply

scintillant nodes

Buffalo beans
Lark buntings

SoDak

stonebones in drywash

coldcamp in sere land

mooncast Badlands

artifacts   ideals   dogtooth
spars   native   US

natural formations

if money is
sacred
the Black Hills still are

WY

        handsome leathery elderly ladies of

Lusk

        between Deadwood and Cheyenne orient

us

        putting in crop   recalling

        bean farmers in Fort Laramie's saloon
                  hunch and grin

CO
down in Denver among silver limpets, najas

fish around his shins
                                          Crivelli's
                Christopher   relieves us

   We followed the blue road in the antique Rand McNally
whithersoever, regardless of more recent constructions. True, the
gate spanning the road posted
                    ADMITTANCE RESTRICTED
and, more blithe than obedient, we gave it short pause. It only
took *Security* a half mile anyway to pull us over and turn us back,
acknowledging nothing of the blue road on our map.

   Down the road at the *Loaf&Jug* the girl explains. "Martin-
Marietta? oh, they make missiles&stuff in there…"

We never saw over that hill.

The Kid's double-action   *Rye*
$15. 1880 .41 Thunderer

white arms red finery hard arts gone under glass

travelling mercies

                                    Ute
                  blessing at Fort

                  Garland

New Mexico

           they flip each other
               the bird
               Memorial Day

          bikers at Taos
                  and pilgrims
              up the Lawrence shrine

"… my vice." his knees

Salazar, the Santero,
          carves a dove against a board in his lap in
the dim hacienda

dead on the lintel of the Cathedral
of Saint Francis at Santa Fe
                a pigeon

hitcher in ditch sits unseeing
head on crossed knees vultures high
wheeling

                         Clines Corners

      PALS
       buried among
unsung Navajo ghosts
      Apache
     ghost prayers sung

                    commemorate
Sumner's multiple legal murders

flowering cholla   flowering yucca
mesquite   saltbush   alligator juniper
's lee   in the wild sultry wind   safe
sleep and sex

we'll be alone at the Bottomless Lakes   *Roswell*

Freetail bats and the poorest tourists
in the rusty truck among fancy campers

let the tarantula have at them
the Cactus wrens emblem us   *Whites City*

3 miles   a half day   750 feet
down the Cavern
                    pupils dilate

for splendour's increase
                sacrifice to subterranean
                            pavement

Broad-tailed hummingbird perches knuckles
fingertip   platerim radish tomato   tentguy
beak taps a fingernail   beak tip   mannerly
long probe into beerbottle   hovers at open
eye   which manoeuvre I watch unflinching
thrills a nostril   darts around to left ear
too much   despite myself   I do
flinch and he whirrs away

cicadas shrill daylong   myriad
clickings in piñons   at dusk
vast squadronic drone   come
morning, beetle tracks in all the dust

waking in the orange nylon puptent
:   waking inside a litebulb

Peter Hurd, Henriette Wyeth
Carolyn's *Open Door*, Clint
Meigs and Johnny, père:

Lincoln Tinney Hondo
San Patricio Ruidoso Capitan

68

bats in the guesthouse eaves
stack scat and click in chinks

the further blessing of empty backroads

scarce Whiptail lizard where feed 10 head / section

Gran Quivira   left in precious
                       little peace

                       disrupted encroached
                           coerced inveigled

remorseless   the never shriven sin and tragedy

I must do stand my wounds in hard light

                                        Mountainair
                                     Albuquerque
                                           Grants

via black malpais   drive back due south

to see who lived at Gila Cliff

who in Silver City: Mark Johns,
Dennis O'Keefe, gentlemen!   I could,
and go to the good   and never
travel more

but go on as
the Mogollon

Prickly-poppy's doeskin petals

brakestink in heat of day

so climbs and drops the road

how comes Wolf spider to die
prone in the trail?

how comes Jane Horst
to Doc's Hot Springs from
Texas?

how we by La Cañada?

then cattle and drovers drank sweet water

Datil Well

and now

Magdalena

radio telescopes spectral in grassland

cut Quemado through Pietown
by sandy track 30 miles
before sandstone Ventana and
swallows' salutatory fly-past

Acoma privacies   two beauteous
                    crones

I never saw a Rattler till I found one in the road:

it writhes yet in the rearview mirror   tying
itself in knots   dying, brother

poorass Gallup

the wealth of squashblossoms
on Crownpoint bosoms

arid land so vital

all I hear is the chat   *Chaco Canyon*
of my own people, and its correlative

— contrail—silence —

but dancing in step   *Pueblo Bonito*
with the skink successfully
she doesn't flee
so fast

CO

from Bisti's hogans via
Durango's fronts to Ouray's
Victoriana, the San Juans, and on
to beaver lodges among the aspens

WY

at Freeman above Baggs which Robert
LeRoy Parker and Longabaugh shot up

I see from Rawlins jail cell window at last
how Earl Durand couldn't've,
those mountains that he loved,
and why he made his break
and was bound to be killed by civilization's hand

crisscrossing the Oregon Trail

riding the Divide   the route
the Pony Express sped   Split
Rock   Ice Slough   surviving

full moon unseen deep   *Popo Agie*
as we be in Sinks Canyon

all the roar I hear
is raw beauty   even
200 years too late

Azures & Swallowtails

it hurts to look over Zion
with a cold eye, that dreamed
locale of the heart
so clearly imagined   found so
            bolloxed

Tetons
wilderness is history   my dream
                        cold scent

Cody got
the last of its best

most elegant wide-awakes in the West
ranged on crowns at the bar in the Irma,
his be-
quest

edifying
          the mountains back-
wards in the rear-
                    view mirror

MT

solstice at the headwaters of the Missouri

Three Forks

dead *Lewis and Clark Vodka* soldier
tossed on the lawn of the bank

"M"

Helena

orientalia and beehives
preserved on the branch
decorate the Last Chance
Gulch Confectionery—

the counterman,
    "Well,
after the first sharp frost
the leaves start fallin' off the bushes
and then you can find 'em
them waspnests
so then the trick is to get 'em home
& put it in the freezer
& then you let it warm back up a little bit
& when the wasps come out they're groggy
& you can hit 'em easy with the flyswatter.
       Once
     when I was a kid
there was a real tough Indi'n bar down here
& we got a nest in a big paper sack
& we shook it up real good & we threw it in there:

yellowjackets and redskins comin' outta 2nd
storey windows…"

Oct 13
1912
Great Falls Mont

Friend Guy

    I came west 31 years ago   at that
time baring the Indians and fiew scaterd
whites the country belonged to God but
now the real estate man an nester have got
moste of it grass side down
    In tame country on a good road an
autos all right but if your hunting for aney
thing wilder than a Doctor take a horse
    well Guy I hope you git a cross all
right and show them Cliff dwelers the real
thing
    well guy I close with best regards to
your self and Wife

                   Your friend
                   CM Russell

ID

up above the Hi-Line:

scumbled distance.

18 May—4 July 1989
Verwood, Saskatchewan

Postface

These four extended efforts, conceived to be more voluminous than they ever wind up, written through my 30s, comprise—together with *Further than the Blood*—all I cared to be responsible for *aetat.* 60. I revise them here as much as they'll let me—not intending to impose tired old-guy values, but touching punctuation, lineation, word choice; allowing, where inalterable, native disjunction and younger nerve while enhancing readability, as it seems to me now, pushing 70.

Blood collected all that seemed worth preserving to 2010. Three of these series were excerpted therein in short single pages, to leave sign of 'em. I venture to resuscitate all four here in their entireties. For *Blood*, *Grandmother* wouldn't sample at all. But I would perpetuate her honour. Her series mediates between the Unattainable States of America and ourselves. *Shownman* is simply the fascinated tale of a proto-environmentalist scuttled by correctitude. *Cold Mine* is composed family bio—no principal, nor reader, to abash. *Travelling Mercies* is by a map that did not quite lead to utopia, surprise-surprise.

May they outlive me. What are the odds.

GB
Victoria, BC

The Author

Guy Birchard began, lives presently, and appears not about but bound to end in Canada.

www.ingramcontent.com/pod-product-compliance
Lightning Source LLC
Chambersburg PA
CBHW031931080426
42734CB00007B/628